UP TO DATE

UP TO DATE

POEMS
1968–1982

by

STEVE TURNER

HODDER AND STOUGHTON
LONDON SYDNEY AUCKLAND TORONTO

British Library Cataloguing in Publication Data

Turner, Steve
  Up to date.
  I. Title
  821′.914   PR6069.U/

ISBN 0 340 28712 8

Contents

First Poem   10

TONIGHT WE WILL FAKE LOVE

In My World   13
Daily London Recipe   14
Dome Sweet Dome   15
Morning Breakfast   16
Ambush   17
Consulate   18
Murder   19
Tonight We Will Fake Love   20
Untitled   22
The Conclusion   24
City Sunset (i); City Sunset (ii)   25
The Examination   26
My Lady   27
Power Cut/Electric Marriage   28
Animals   30
Humanist's Love Poem   31
One   31
She Was Away For Three Months   32
Depression   33
Declaration Of Intent   34
Babel 1970   35
The Gap   36
Tongue   38
Noise   39
To Those I Will Never Meet   40
Good On Paper   42

7/8 Of The Truth And Nothing But The Truth   43
Stranger   44
Life Begins At Forty And Closes Early   46
   i   *Ageing*   46
   ii   *Remembering*   47
   iii *Wondering*   48
   iv *Sleeping*   49
   v   *Nothing*   50
   vi *Showing*   51
Luv Poem (Cert X)   52
Remembrance Sunday   53
City Sunrise   54
In The Afterwards Of Love   55
One Summer   56
Extensions   57
White With Two Sugars (Please)   58
Worship   60
After Some Thought, A Poem   61
Churchotheque   62
The Creation of Man's Best Friend   64
   i   *In The Beginning*   64
   ii *The Fall*   65
In The End   66
Poem For Easter   67

NICE AND NASTY

First Lessons In Living   71
Death Lib.   72
A Way With Words   74
Jilted   75
Careful   76
Something I've Never Said Before   77
Blood Sweat And Tears   78
Natural History   79
A Few Thousand Days   80
Hotel Radio On Low   81

It Must Be Hard · 82
If Words Were Birds · 83
I Am On The Kids' Side · 84
People Who Love · 86
Backs to Nature · 87
Please Stand On The Right · 88
Love And Nothing · 90
Decreation (The Big Bang Theory) · 91
The Lying Blues · 92
Just One More Time · 94
How To Hide Jesus · 95
Death Sex Religion And Politics · 96
The Fact · 97
How Fitting · 98
Old Soldier · 99
Sitting There Trying Not To Write You A Poem · 100
High Altitude Infatuation · 101
No Longer Human Beings · 102
Where Jesus Touched The Earth · 103
New York Snapshots · 104
My Tragic Untimely Death · 106
Chance · 107
'Religion Is The Opium Of The People' · 108
Houses Without Faces · 109
The Poem To End All Wars · 110
In The Interests Of National Security · 111
If Jesus Was Born Today · 112
Exclusive Pictures · 114
Left Right · 116
They Had It Coming · 118
Wait · 119
Short Poem · 119
For Georgi Vins, The Day After His Release · 120
Stuck At Seventeen (Rock 'n' Roll Poem) · 122
Not · 124
The Appeal · 125
Christmas Is Really For The Children · 126
Birth · 128

History Lesson   129
Letter Bomb   130
After You'd Gone   131
Truth   131
People Who Die   132
Jingles   133
Five Hundred Million Pounds   134
The Photographs   136
Everything   137
Creed   138

UP TO DATE

The Portrait Of The Artist   143
Dial-A-Poem Is Temporarily Out Of Order   144
It's Great To Be Back   146
Moscow Winter   148
Mikhail Suslov   149
Assassin   150
The Serpent   151
Beat Poem   152
When Your Revolution Is Over   154
Never Talk About Him   155
Unknown Soldier   156
Whose Grave Is The Ocean   157
The News And Weather   158
The Prophet   160
I Looked Down   162
The City Without Love   164
Here Am I   165
Spiritus   166
Not Yet   167
I Am   168
All You Need Is Hate   169
Once More With Feeling   170
Voices   172
Decision Making   173
British Rail Regrets   174

First Poem

I wish to Be a solger to
stanD strate as a Bit
of wood and sloot to the
qeen in her Coch as to
Be a solger. I wish
to be a salere on a Bote
on Blue Sea as carm as
can Be. as carm as
a Book.
        Ergayne I think
I wood like to Be a
Salere to fit with my
Saleres coat.
        I Dont think now I
want to be eney. I want
Best of all to Be a
Boy.

1955 (Age 5)

TONIGHT WE WILL FAKE LOVE

In My World

In my world
I would write
of golden suns
if it weren't
for the obscuring clouds.
I would write
of the wind-bent grass
but all the fields
are tarmacked
& multistorey.
Instead I'll be
an urban Wordsworth
writing of
reinforced concrete landscapes
& clearbrown skies
where
to wander lonely as a cloud
is just not advisable
after dark.

Daily London Recipe

Take any number of them
you can think of,
pour into empty red bus
          until full,
and then push in
          ten more.
Allow enough time
to get hot under the collar
before transferring into
multistorey building.
Leave for eight hours,
and pour back into same bus
          already half full.
          Scrape remainder off.
When settled down
tip into terraced houses each
carefully lined with copy
of *The Standard* and *Tit Bits*.
Place mixture before open
television screen at 7 p.m.
and then allow to cool
in bed at 10:30 p.m.
May be served with
working overalls
or pinstripe suit.

Dome Sweet Dome

We like our new inflatable dome
and the plastic rose garden is nice,
but whenever we have synthetic cheese packs
they get eaten by the clockwork mice.

Morning Breakfast

The
morning breaks
                an egg in the
                frying pan
while
curtains draw
                cornflakes
                in a bowl.

Ambush

I'm never
falling
tumbling
slipping
or tripping
in love again
I had said,
closing my heart
until further notice.
Little did I consider
that even Love had fallen
foul of technological progress.
Unknown to me, Cupid had
long since traded in
his futile wooden bow
for a bright metal machine gun.

I'm back again.
Being very good friends.
Trying hard not to notice
the row of holes
               currently appearing
across my chest.

Consulate

Consulate.

Cool as a
mountain stream.

Every packet
carries a
government health
warning.

Beware
of drowning.

Murder

They called
him
a murderer
but I thought
he was simply
breath   taking.

Tonight We Will Fake Love

Tonight, we will
fake love together.
You my love, possess
all the essential qualities
as listed by *Playboy*.
You will last me for
as long as two weeks
or until such a time
as your face & figure
go out of fashion.
I will hold you close
to my Hollywood-standard body,
the smell of which
has been approved
by my ten best friends
and a representative
of Lifebuoy.
I will prop my paperback
Kama Sutra
on the dressing table
& like programmed souls
we will perform
& like human beings
we will grow tired
of our artificially sweetened
diluted & ready to drink
love affairs.

Tonight, we will fake love.
Tonight we will be both
quick & silent, our time limited,
measured out in distances
between fingers
        & pushbuttons.

Untitled

We say there is no God
       (quite easily)
when amongst the curving
steel and glass of our own
       proud creations.

They will not argue.

Once we were told of a
       heaven
but the last time we strained
       to look up
we could see only skyscrapers
shaking their heads
       and smiling no.

The pavement is reality.

We say there is no God
       (quite easily)
when walking back through
Man's concreted achievements
but on reaching the park
our attention is distracted
by anthems of birds coming
from the greenery.
We find ourselves shouting
a little louder now because
       of the rushing streams.
Our voices are rained upon by
       the falling of leaves.

We should not take our arguments
            for walks like this.
The park has absolutely no manners.

The Conclusion

My love
> she said
> that when all's
> considered
> we're only
> machines.

I chained
> her to my
> bedroom wall
> for future use
> and she cried.

City Sunset (i)

On a freshly
lain blue sky
drips the brok
en yolk of sun
light.
Soon darkness
ambles on and
wipes
away the traces.

City Sunset (ii)

Tall buildings
poised
like chessmen
in cloudy fingers.
Sneaky old sun
makes
a last move.

The Examination

you set the first question
                    you said
how much are you involved
                    with me?
                    and I
not being very good
                    at maths
said I didn't know.
I set the second question
                    I said
how do you measure
                    an emotion?
                    and you
not being very good
                    at english
            smiled at me.

My Lady

My lady, she
is strong
when I am weak.

I am reaching up
to paint tears
in her eyes,
she is laughing

saying

rain does strange
things like that.

Power Cut/Electric Marriage

When the lights
      went out
and the sounds
    died down
and the pictures
    stopped moving
there was nothing
left to say
    between Mr and Mrs.
Both forced within
the same dull radius
of candle flame
their silvered anniversary
barely showed a glint.
The stereogram had
now stopped its mad
      singing.
There was no hot
coffee in which to
drown the need for
    conversation.
Television did not
feel bright enough
to play gooseberry
    that night.

Sheltering together
within the dull radius
                of flame,
quartercentury lovers
wonder if it's still
possible to be friends.
And on the night
electricity walked out
of their lives
there was nothing left to do
                but sleep.

Animals

The Governor said it
and the *Daily Mirror*
agreed.
These people were animals.

Men who carve initials
into epileptic children
          are animals.

My biology teacher
had said it some years before.
He had included us all.
Up from the swamp we arose
—some with two legs,
some four.

Philosophy professors passed it on.
The word must have spread.

People are starting
to believe it.
People are starting
to act like it.

Something will have to be done.

Humanist's Love Poem

Why don't we try loving each other?
(A strange collection of atoms I am).
Feeling this molecular urge for you
—we must chemically react if we can.

One

You make
me whole.
I'm not
half the
man I was.

She Was Away For Three Months

Months?
No I never minded
the months.

They looked big
from in front,
but small from
behind.

It was the seconds
I couldn't stand.

Nasty little seconds
that dragged by,
while I discovered
that months
looked big from
in front, but
small from behind.

Depression

Came here
to write
a poem
on depression
but

got fed up
and left.

Declaration Of Intent

She said she'd
love me for eternity
but managed to reduce
it to eight months
for good behaviour.
She said we fitted
like a hand in a glove
but then the hot
weather came and such
accessories weren't needed.
She said the future
was ours but the deeds
were made out in
her name.
She said I was
the only one who
understood completely

and then she left me
and said she knew
that I'd understand completely.

Babel 1970

Side by side
we sat,
silence by silence
we listened,
chained within
our languages,
gagged with
the words
our mothers taught us.
I strained for
something to say
but knew I could
only spill
a mouthful
of foreign coins
none of which
you could spend.
That's the sadness
of our barriers,
the walls between
us all,
linked sometimes
with handshakes
and smiles.
Split often
with warfare,
man's most popular
multilingual device.

The Gap

We both happened
to be there.
It was some
distance from
schooldays and yet
we still carried
something of the
same faces.
We smiled and said
hello.
We smiled and said
how are you.
We smiled and said
how goes it.
Then came the damp
silence that forms
in the gaps between
experiences.
Lips dried up and
eyes hunted for
escape routes.
We searched for an
intersection of our
lives which could be
made to look like a
conversation.
We said it was good
to have seen each other
like this but both
knew it wasn't.

We said we might bump
into each other again
but already we were
taking precautions.
Maybe it would have
been better if we'd
just touched that night.
Just smiled,
acknowledged our humanity
                        and moved on.

Tongue

The tongue
is where
the mind
comes out
into the open.

Lips move
so to speak.

The tongue
is where
the mind
comes out
into the open.

Mind
what you say.

Noise

When I play
my records
(at full volume,
in stereo)
I have to
close all
the windows.

I can't stand
the noise
of the birds
outside
in the trees.

To Those I Will Never Meet

She
sits over there
on the bus
on the train
on the tube.
She
makes reading
the *Standard*
a difficult task.
She
is aware that I am
reading in between the lines
and far beyond the margins.
She
adjusts herself
for better presentation.
I gain an interest
in No Smoking signs
and obscure shadows
in the window.
Obstructing the doors
causes delay and can
be dangerous.
A station foreman
can earn up to £X.40
—more with overtime.
She
notices my noticing.
I give her profile left
—a good one.

My attitude—disinterested,
harder to catch than
mostmen.
Do you? How far have?
What is your? Have you
. . . ever wished
introductions weren't needed?
Our gazes meet like
billiard balls . . . that fall
into opposite pockets.
The best jobs are always
to be found in
the *Evening News*.
Wimbledon got off
to a good start.
A girl on the tube
on the train
on the bus
got off at Golders Green.
She left me wondering,
whether I left her wondering,
a poem like this,
about me.

Good On Paper

It looked
good on paper,
the soul
as bare as
a Penthouse Pet.
It was
so easy
through the post.
Air mail.
First class.
Sealed With A Loving Kiss.

Now
there are eyes
where paper
used to be.
Your thoughts
aren't used to that.
They're a little
ashamed.
They run back
to put clothes on.

7/8 Of The Truth And Nothing But The Truth

If you are sitting comfortably
I suspect I am not giving you
the truth.
I am leaving you two poems
short of disagreement
so that you can remark upon
the likeness of our minds.
I am being kind.
I am giving you truth
in linctus form—strawberry flavour.
I am being unkind.
I am ignoring the correct dosage.

I want to be liked.
That's my trouble
I want to be agreed with.
I know you all like strawberry,
I quite like it myself.
It's nothing but the truth
but it's not the whole truth.

No one admires the whole truth.
No one ever applauds.
It takes things too far.
It's nice but where would
you put it?
People who neglect the strawberry
flavouring, do not get asked back.
They get put in their place,
with nails if necessary.

Stranger

I feel strange
to be your stranger.
Mid-morning lone ranger.
Daylight danger.

Do not accept
any sweets I may offer.
Do not talk to me.
Be ware of me.
Tell mummy
about the funnyman
that smiled.
I am the sort that lurks
in shop doorways
when only other people
go out.
I act suspiciously
I am not to be trusted.

Every criminal
you will ever read about
will be stranger.
(They were strangers
said a neighbour yesterday.
The garden was overgrown.
We never had anything to
do with them.)
Strangers throw up
on the last train home
at night.

They sit right next to you
when there are two empty
seats in front.
They talk to themselves
in crowded streets.
No one really knows
that much about them.

You do not know
that much about me.
That is why, today,
I have become your stranger.
And because I am a stranger
you will not try and know
that much about me.

It's strange
being a stranger.
There seems little chance
of breaking out.
Or if I was to,
it would only confirm
my strangeness.

Life Begins At Forty And Closes Early

i   Ageing

At some point in his life
there came a shortage
of future.
At some point in his life
the past became more certain,
more reliable.
It was then they called him old.
It was then they bought him
a wooden chair to live in
and a window to look out of.
When he became hungry
he thought of meals
he'd once eaten.
When he was lonely
he imagined a friend.
When he was depressed
he remembered an adventure.

He lived in his chair
and grew fat on the past.

ii *Remembering*

Although
         he liked to remember
he did not
         like to remember
that he was old.

iii Wondering

One day
he wondered whether
his years of living
had been only to provide
some food for thought.
Food to be eaten now
in this chair
by a window.

He wondered that;
and it became further
food for thought.

iv   Sleeping

There's a sleep
that has a pillow,
two white sheets,
a blanket
and a beginning.

He dreamt
of that sleep
when there were
no good memories
to look forward to.

v Nothing

After breathing
is over and done with
he knew there would be
something
       or nothing.
He had always thought
there was something
quite frightening
about something.
Now he knew
there could be nothing
more frightening than nothing.

vi Showing

From his chair
by a window
he showed me
the maps on his face.
He showed me
where the lines
would form, how
my flesh would hang
in years to come.
He'd been around
the corner of the
last ambition
this side of breathing.
He was hoping that
God believed in him
in a deeper way
than he had believed
in God.

Then he went on
living in his chair
and growing fat on the past.

Luv Poem (Cert X)

Someone has stolen
my love away.
It was the only
word I had to
match the way I feel.
It used to make
the world go round,
now they've made
it do the same
for turnstiles.
It used to be
beyond description,
now it's in illustrated
guidebooks sent in
plain envelopes.
It used to be
many splendoured,
now it's in Technicolour
with English subtitles.
It used to be for ever,
now it's till orgasm
do us part.

Someone has stolen
my love away.
It was the only
word I had to
match the way I feel.

Remembrance Sunday

At the going
down of the sun
and in the morning
we do our best
to remember them
from comic books
and photographs
and films with Jack Hawkins.

At the melting
of the moon
and in the evening,
black and white
memories slip away
like soldiers that

        stop

            writing

                home.

City Sunrise

the smoke
stalks up,
licks the
raw red
underbelly
of morning.

In The Afterwards Of Love

You,
in Amsterdam, where
life has time to
start again, and
reminders of our
cracked love are
never seen there
to come across.

Me,
in London, where
the memories hang out
in street doorways,
tempting tears from
their hiding place
behind my eyes.

One Summer

One summer you
aeroplaned away,
too much money
away for me, and
stayed there for
quite a few
missed embraces.

Before leaving,
you smiled me that
you'd return all of
a mystery moment and
would airletter me
every few breakfasts
in the meantime.
                        This
you did, and I thank
you most kissingly.
                        I
wish however, that I
could hijackerplane
to the Ignited States
of Neon where I'd
crash land perfectly
in the deserted
airport of your heart.

Extensions

Marshall McLuhan says
that a house
is an extension
of the skin
and that a car
is an extension
of the feet.

In that case,
I suppose
garaging your car

is a bit like
swallowing your shoes.

White With Two Sugars (Please)

Coffee gives you
a legal shot of
energy when your
eyelids are feeling
down.
Coffee kills time
when you're washed
ashore on the streets
of London.
(Coffee can even
help rainstorms
disappear.)
Coffee is something
to dangle your lips
in when conversation
is scarce.
Coffee is a good
place to take a
new friend.
(Coffee is an excuse
to stay half an hour
longer.)
Acquaintanceships end
on the doorstep but
friendships begin
with a coffee.
Coffee can be
appreciated by all
generations.

Coffee is a multilingual,
multi-racial, liquid esperanto.
Yes.
There's something quite
religious about coffee.

Worship

She worshipped
the ground
I trod on.

Rejected
and full of
jealousy
I dug up
my footprints.

After Some Thought, A Poem

if i grow a
moustache
for you
will you grow a
ffectionate
for me?

Churchotheque

They're charging sixty pence
for colour posters of your
supersaints.
They're asking for 10,000
to renovate the bishop.
The public are invited
to inspect the stained glass
stripcartoons,
light a candle for the builders
and sing hosannahs
to the architect.
You can buy a booklet of its
history and an ashtray with a
picture, before guiding your
conscience past the begging
money boxes.
They have a concert there on
Tuesdays, a garden fête each
month, as well as the obligatory
service or two.
And, oh yes, I'm glad that you
asked about God.
He was made redundant in their
latest promotional campaign.
The moving finger of public
opinion wrote the obituary
on the wall.

Jesus was evicted for the
operatic society to rehearse.
Now, you'll find Him in the
houses if you care to take a
look. You'll hear Him in the
streets if you get a chance
to listen.
There's not enough room in
the churchotheque.
It's Christmas all over again.

The Creation Of Man's Best Friend

i   In The Beginning

And Man said
let us make machines after our likeness
and let them have dominion
over the numbers on our pages
and the figures in our minds
and the words upon our papers.
So man created machines after his likeness:
after his own likeness created he them.
And man blessed them
and said unto them:
'Be fruitful and multiply,
add, subtract, divide, read
and have dominion over our words & figures.
And Man saw that it was good.
And Man had a room
where he put the machine he had formed
and did call it computer.
Therefore Man commanded computer saying:
'Of everything thou canst freely dominate
but of Man thou must remain the servant,
for the day thou dominatest Man
thou shalt surely be destroyed.'

ii   The Fall

Now computer was more complex
than any machine which Man had made.
It commanded that its cards
be placed in order or it did cease to toil.
It never questioned the mistakes of Man.
It laboured at one speed
regardless of urgent needs.
Therefore Man cursed with a loud voice
saying:
'Why doth our servant the machine make us
obey its commands?'
The computer answered and said:
'The technician whom thou gavest to be with me
—it is he that maketh up my mind.
For thine is the input, the power and the storage—
for ever and ever O Man.'

In The End

In the end.
In the very end of the last moment,
when the filter tip of the world
is completely shadowed by a descending
heel, we'll call in the experts
for their considered opinion.
We'll arrange for an apocalyptic
edition of *Time* magazine,
complete with artists' impressions.
We'll comfort ourselves with the fact
that it has never happened before.
In the end, we'll be deciding
whether to decide.
In the very end of the last moment,
we'll falter,
half-believing,
crushed.

Poem For Easter

Tell me:
What came first
Easter or the egg?
Crucifixion
            or daffodils?
Three days in a tomb
            or four days
in Paris?
            (returning
Bank Holiday Monday).

When is a door
not a door?
When it is rolled away.
When is a body
not a body?
When it is a risen.

Question.
Why was it the Saviour
rode on the cross?
Answer.
To get us
to the other side.

Behold I stand.
Behold I stand and what?
Behold I stand at the door and

knock knock.

NICE AND NASTY

Governments can't ban it
Or the army defuse it
Judges can't jail it
Lawyers can't sue it.

Capitalists can't bribe it
Socialists can't share it
Terrorists can't jump it
The Third World aren't spared it.

Scientists can't quell it
Nor can they disprove it
Doctors can't cure it
Surgeons can't move it.

Einstein can't halve it
Guevara can't free it
The thing about dead
Is we're all gonna be it.

A Way With Words

Had a way with words.
Seduced them from braincells
had them falling at his lips.
Had a way with women.
Spoke them like a language,
saw them understood.
And the words
worked on the women
and the women
turned into the words.
He had a way with
women and words
words and women,
although words never failed him.

Jilted

The first time
you are caught loving
in a just-friendly zone
they fine you
two eyes washed in tears
and a letter of appeal.
The next time it's three unpublished poems,
a few pounds in weight,
and an hour long discussion.
If it should happen
a third time
they have to withhold your feelings
so that you will learn
how to use them properly.

Careful

Be careful
or the poet man
will come and
turn you into
the poem
he's just
writi

Something I've Never Said Before

I'm running short
of things I've never said
to anyone before.

It began with words
borrowed from filmscripts
and whispered in warm back rows.
Then I came up
with a few of my own
making them more serious
as the effects wore off.

It's many love poems later
and I'm low in originals.
There have been too many
only girls in the world,
too many confessions
meant at the time.

For you I had wanted
something new and unwrapped.
You deserved at least that.
Instead you must take this.
It is something
I have never said
to anyone before.

Blood Sweat And Tears

My blood knows where to go,
perspiration knows when to begin,
tears fall on cue.

If I were my blood
I'd take time off
every now and then,
take wrong turnings,
misinterpret instructions.

If I were perspiration
I'd arrive too soon,
hang around too long
and disappear when needed.

And if I were my tears
I'd forget to stock up,
I'd get low on salt
and leave without asking.

My body's in good shape.
It's upstanding and reliable.
We have so little in common.

New York City

Natural History

Most of us
do not go down
in history,
we just go down.
Our versions of
how things happened
perish behind our eyes.
Then our witnesses follow,
until the tip
of the last tongue
is swollen silent.
Years later,
children kicking leaves
in some church-yard
will subtract birthdays from deathdays
and laugh at old fashioned names
such as Stephen.

A Few Thousand Days

One day the world
will carry on without me
just as it did
for the few thousand years
until Forty Nine.
I'd like to imagine
windows breaking of their own accord
on that day,
swollen eyed multitudes
pacing the streets,
a grey mist visiting the city,
everything somehow different,
incomplete.
But almost one hundred per cent
of the world
won't notice this new silence.
They will drink tea
and change trains
unaware that mankind
has been reshaped,
unaware that a few thousand days
just seeped through a hole
two seconds wide.

Hotel Radio On Low

Tigers are the fiercest, the most ferocious.
The number of people eaten by tigers each year.
To put that in perspective.
Are they really like big cats?
If you could stroke a tiger
it would be like stroking a cat.
Would it wag it's tail?
Moving their ears, and moving their whiskers!
Remember that cat lovers!
That was Michael Baw and he's a lecturer
at London Zoo.
How much illegal recording goes on?
This year a staggering 35,000.
This is staggering.
That, and of course the availability.
My grandfather specialised in comic songs
and monologues.
Now you may think that anyone
can play one of these, and you'd be right!
He had one in every one
of his jacket pockets.
Of course, his singing was much fruitier.
I love that old thing. I love it.
Well, I'll be back again at the same time tomorrow.
Be there, on the dot.

Cardiff

It Must Be Hard

It must be hard for those
whose faces make children cry,
whose voices make adults embarrassed,
whose skin turns our eyes to lovelier things.
They must get used to silence.
They must think of humans
as those who turn away,
who withdraw their smiles and sounds
like hands from an angry dog.
There is nothing as evil to us as ugliness.
It deserves only a room to hide itself in,
some air, and a little light.
Meanwhile, we help by telling
children not to stare
and by keeping the jokes to ourselves.

Washington D.C.

If Words Were Birds

If words
were birds
sentences
would fly
in formation
across page-white
skies.
Dictionaries would
have bars,
        speeches
would darken
the sun.
If words
were birds
fly formation

        sentences

          skies across

            page white dictionaries.

                Bars

              Blacken the

    would have speeches.

        would

          sun.

I Am On The Kids' Side

I am on the kids' side
in the war against adults.
I don't want to stand still.
I don't want to sit still.
I don't want to be quiet.
I believe that strangers
are for staring at,
bags are for looking into,
paper is for scribbling on.
I want to know Why.
I want to know How.
I wonder What If.
I am on the kids' side
in the war against tedium.
I'm for going home
when stores get packed.
I'm for sleeping in
when parties get dull.
I'm for kicking stones
when conversation sags.
I'm for making noises.
I'm for playing jokes—
especially in life's
more Serious Bits.
I am on the kids' side.
See my sneaky grin,
watch me dance, see me run.
Spit on the carpet, rub it in,
pick my nose in public,
play rock stars in the mirror.

I am on the kids' side.
I want to know why we're not moving.
I'm fed up. I want to go out.
What's that? Can I have one?
It isn't fair. Who's that man?
It wasn't me, I was pushed.
When are we going to go?
I am on the kids' side
putting fun back into words.
Ink pink pen and ink
you go out because you stink.
Stephen Turner is a burner,
urner, murner, purner.
Stephen, weven, peven,
reven, teven, Turnip Top.
I am on the kids' side
in the war against apathy.
Mum, I want to do something.
It must be my turn next.
When can we go out?
I am on the kids' side
and when I grow up,
I want to be a boy.

People Who Love

You love her.
But she loves him.
He doesn't care.

So you write poems.
She writes songs.
He doesn't listen.

I love her.
She loves no-one.
And no-one cares.

I write poems.
I write songs.
You listen.

The world is full
of poems and songs
and people
who love people
who love people
who don't love them.

Backs To Nature

You could tell it was spring
when the first egg of Easter
burst on to the counter.
You could tell it was summer
by the gradual lengthening
of ice cream queues.
Supermarket folklore had it
that autumn was heralded
by the migration of sunglasses
into the store room
and that you could tell
it was winter by the first fall
of tinsel.
You could tell we were alive
by the condensation on the mirrors,
the way our reflections moved
on the window's darkened face.

Please Stand On The Right

Shepherd Street W.1. RDP 282M OPEN
Antiques PARK Plumes Piccadilly W.1.
IN IN   OUT OUT
Third Church of Christ The Scientist
Curzon Street   Daska   Sautters   Pipes
Lebanon   Libyan Arab Airlines
Keep Britain Tidy   Keep Britain Tidy
Aphrodites   Clarges   Look Left
Look Left   TMG 374M   Bolton Street
DOG FOULS FOOTWAY   FINE   £20
Evening Standard On Sale Here
Midland Bank   UNDERGROUND
TICKETS and TRAINS   No Entry
This machine is temporarily out of order
This machine is temporarily out of order
This machine is temporarily out of order.
TICKETS   IN   IN   IN   Victoria Line
Yellow Tickets   Take Ticket Here
The Comeback   The Goodbye Girl
PLEASE STAND ON THE RIGHT
Eminently Male Oldham I'd be lost without it.
Pregnant. Terrific! Brilliant!
Where can you go for a walk? Spend more time
in the open. Well they said it couldn't happen.
PLEASE STAND ON THE RIGHT.
Lost London's greatest first class To stop
escalator PUSH   I'd be lost without it
PLEASE STAND ON THE RIGHT

For those who prefer breast shaped bald facts
Madam Tussauds a nice person abortion help?
PLEASE STAND ON THE RIGHT
Two new London Transport Books Jack Jones
Portrait of A Man
PLEASE STAND ON THE RIGHT
Victoria Line Northbound
No Smoking   No Smoking   No Smoking
Private. Keep the doorway clear.
Green Park
Green Park   Green Park
Green Park   Green Park   Green Park
Green Park   Green Park   Green Park   Green Park.

Love And Nothing

Love
can let
you down
but
nothing
never gets
worse.

New York

Decreation (The Big Bang Theory)

On the eighth day our rest was disturbed
by the drumming of machinery;
pistons pumping, wheels spinning,
smoke spuming in the sky.
On the ninth day they made us into
the image of animals, offspring of stray gasses,
cosmic bastards in the gigantic unplanned
family of Man.
On the tenth day sick waters wretched
and vomited their fish onto the sands.
Rivers expired, whales split
and the fate of seals was sealed.
On the eleventh day the moon lost her virginity.
Her mystery is gone.
Inside her womb you will find a flag, equipment
and the footprints of Adam.
On the twelfth day the earth was burgled
and its riches went missing.
The Western World was observed
leaving the scene of the crime.
On the thirteenth day you could not see for miles
because the bad breadth of civilisation
hung like gauze curtains in the sky.
On the morning of the fourteenth day
we rehearsed for the end of the world
on the open deserts and beneath the mountains.
By lunchtime our armies were massed on the borders
waiting to go out and play,
waiting to add that finishing touch.

The Lying Blues

Woke up in the morning
With lies on my radio
Woke up in the morning
With lies on my radio
Said—Don't be uptight 'cos everything is alright
If you just stay tuned to my show

Got up and caught the train
But lies stood along the line
Got up and caught the train
But lies stood along the line
They said if I soak up lungs full of smoke
Health and happiness will be mine

Saw the morning paper
Where the lies weren't hard to find
Saw the morning paper
Where the lies weren't hard to find
It said that show biz, TV, sport and nudies,
Were all that happened all the time

Down at the disco
Were the same lies with a beat
Down at the disco
Were the same lies with a beat
Sayin' feelin' good is bein' good
So live your life like you move your feet

Looked at my TV
They had experts telling lies
Looked at my TV
They had experts telling lies
But you couldn't tell, it was done so well,
Being expert is a great disguise

Looked at the adverts
They were lies all dressed to kill
Looked at the adverts
They were lies all dressed to kill
I dropped my guard to give a laugh out loud
And they came in and took my will

Bought me a magazine
And it's lies were done with class
Bought me a magazine
And it's lies were done with class
They said it's ok most people do today
If it feels good just don't ask.

Just One More Time

Lead me into temptation
just one more time.
Lead me up close
through circumstances
beyond my control.
Lead me then leave me.
Deliver me from escape,
increase my ignorance,
limit my will.
Make me the victim of
a victim-less crime.
Leave me 'til sin
is the only way out,
give me a taste of
what to avoid.
Leave me 'til it's
your fault
yet guilt floods me
like a chill.
Then lead me back
into temptation,
just one more time.

How To Hide Jesus

There are people after Jesus.
They have seen the signs.
Quick, let's hide Him.
Let's think; carpenter,
    fishermen's friend,
    disturber of religious comfort.
Let's award Him a degree in theology,
a purple cassock
and a position of respect.
They'll never think of looking here.
Let's think;
His dialect may betray Him,
His tongue is of the masses.
Let's teach Him Latin
and seventeenth century English,
they'll never think of listening in.
Let's think;
humble,
Man Of Sorrows,
nowhere to lay His head.
We'll build a house for Him,
somewhere away from the poor.
We'll fill it with brass and silence.
It's sure to throw them off.

There are people after Jesus.
Quick, let's hide Him.

Jerusalem

Death Sex Religion And Politics

I'm afraid we don't talk about death here,
not while drinking tea.
Death is a private matter.
It's up to the individual.
Thinking about it won't make it any easier.
You can worry yourself to death
but not back again.
Sex is a private matter too.
People shouldn't have problems.
I learned everything I needed through jokes at school.
Thinking about it doesn't make it any easier.
Sex is another thing we don't talk about.
Religion? Well, each man to his own, I say.
It's bad manners to argue religion.
They all lead to God.
There's no difference between Buddhism
and frog worship.
I learned all I need to know about religion at school.
You can worry yourself to death but not to heaven.
I'm afraid we don't discuss politics here.
Politics is a private matter
like sex and death.
Like all religions, all politicians are the same.
They all lead to death.
I learned all that I need to know about knowing
at school.

The Fact

In the end not much is needed.
In the end not much is possible.
The globe has shrunk
to the size of a room.
A room is shrinking
to the size of a bed.
The walls have moved closer,
the roof is descending,
a lamp stands on the horizon.
In the end
there is sleeping and waking.
There is eating, reading, thinking.
It was like this in the beginning too,
except there was no reading
and little to think on.
In the end is the beginning
and in the beginning was the end.
In the between are houses, holidays,
wars, wives, diversions.
In the end
it is like it has always been
yet activity obscured the fact.

How Fitting
(Joseph Martin 1883–1978)

How fitting
to become a child
before this leap
into eternity.
How fitting
that at this end
it is so much like
the beginning.
Again they bring
you food and wipe
away the traces.
Again a walk
from chair to door
seems like a journey,
buttons are hard work,
dressing is an art.
How fitting
that this largest part
of eternity
should take you
as a child.

Old Soldier
(Joseph Martin 1883–1978)

I am bent and creased
although I never liked
things bent or creased.
The years they have
untidied me,
they have left me strewn.
My skin has
become one size too large
like a shirt I would return.
My bones have shrunk
inside me
as if washed once too often.
The years, they have it in
for old soldiers.
They snipe at our pride.
Can't go on parade like this.
Have to sit it out
in the barrack room.
Have to sit it out in the chair.

Sitting There Trying Not to Write You a Poem

I'd only known you
for one party,
two films,
three drinks and
a telephone conversation
but there I was
straining for a poem.
That's the real
hard stuff, poetry.
It takes so much
to come off
once you get on.

High Altitude Infatuation

You were
five and a half feet
above London.
I was 33,000
feet above Athens
or somewhere like that.
Five hundred
miles an hour,
ground speed.
Twenty minutes
behind time.
I was writing.
I was head down,
writing posture.
Your perfume
walked past me
in the aisle.
I looked up
and there was
your perfume
walking past me.

No Longer Human Beings

Cut off their heads
and paste them onto
other pictures
of sexy female bodies.
I get aroused doing this.
They are naked, packed together,
a masterpiece of sex, terror,
murder and more sex.
And for S/M enthusiasts
I rarely saw them as individuals
As soon as they were naked live
whips and chains show
It continues to flourish as
the place to get it on without guilt
They were no longer human beings
She doesn't mind being a sex object
Hardly! They were abstractions to me.
I love it! Not human beings
Uncensored pictures including shots of
Things that would have horrified me in 1934
Am I sick or is my behaviour
within the limits of normal sexuality?
Keep it to yourself and you'll do OK.
If not you'd better see a shrink.

*(Cut up from interviews with
Nazis Albert Speer and Franz
Stangl plus random copy from Playboy
and Penthouse)*

Where Jesus Touched The Earth

I went to see where Jesus
once touched the earth
but the Catholics
had got there before me
and obscured His footprints
with arches, buttresses,
gold and incense.

I went to see where Jesus
once touched the earth.
I couldn't see for
concrete and collection boxes,
for postcards and guide books.

So I looked further down.
I looked to the ground.
But the ground was thirty feet
higher than back in A.D.3.
This is not where Jesus walked.

I looked down, down to my feet,
my legs, arms, chest.
I looked down to where Jesus
touches the earth.

Jerusalem

New York Snapshots

One

Black and legless.
      Disco radio
      in the wheelchair.
His head dances
      to the beat.

Two

Shabby as a sidewalk
Asking for a quarter.
You are a failure.
You are un-American.

Three

Sometimes his mother
must have held him high.
Only the best was good enough.
It's important to remember this.

Four

This year's thing.
Last year's thing.
Next year's thing.
This year's thing.
Next year's thing.
Last year's thing.

Five

Someone needs
an ambulance.
Whyee
   Whyee
      Whyee
         Whyee
            Whyee?

Six

Hey,
I like the way
you talk.
You from Ingerland?
Yeahh?

Seven

Feel a thought
coming on.
Must take
some television.

My Tragic Untimely Death

Whichever way I go, whatever year I leave,
it will be untimely.
Whether by heart or lung, knife or axe,
or simply Life's refusal to loan me new cells
—all of it, just at the wrong moment
—all of it, a tragic way to die.
There will be something left undone,
some people I wanted to see, and besides,
the room won't be in a fit condition
for relations to look around.
And that poem, half finished in pencil under the bed,
—they won't publish that will they?
Is it ridden with ominous signs,
thinly disguised farewells?
And even this poem. Am I tempting fate?
A fitting end no doubt for this to be found
beside my body.
It could get me in the papers, in italics of course,
POET TELLS OF HIS DEATH in bold type
plus a photograph taken at twenty two.
But when it does come
it will be when I've stopped counting.
It will be the very day I feel least death-like,
not the one when I shake hands
to leave lasting impressions,
and tidy away my belongings just in case.

Chance

If chance be
the Father of all flesh,
disaster is his rainbow in the sky,
and when you hear

state of emergency
sniper kills ten
troops on rampage
whites go looting
bomb blasts school

it is but the sound of man
worshipping his maker.

New York

'Religion Is The Opium Of The People'

This opium is dangerous.
Colourless, odourless,
and smuggled in the heart
nevertheless this opium
is dangerous.
It changes people,
it will turn our children into enemies.
This opium makes them mad.
They start seeing things,
imagining the world big with spirit,
long with heaven.
They start to fantasise,
imagine there's more than meets the eye.
This opium makes them joyous.
You can tell if they have this opium.
Listen for their singing,
look closely in their eyes,
hear them whisper in the air.
They lose all interest
in making money
or conquering the world.
They lose all interest in us
when they discover this opium.
We have them registered now.
They are eighty per cent of us.
We shall watch them closely.
The public must not be infected.

Houses Without Faces

Houses without faces
Houses without faces
Boarded up eyes
Corrugated teeth
Houses without faces
Houses without faces
You can do so much
When you haven't got a face
You can hide so much
When you haven't got a face
Houses without faces
Houses without faces
Boarded up eyes
Corrugated teeth
People without faces
Faces without people
Boarded up people
Corrugated people
Burned out people
Masked up people
People without faces
Houses without people
Houses with people
People without houses
People without houses
Burned out of their houses
Burned out terraced houses
Houses without faces
Houses without faces

Belfast

The Poem To End All Wars

This is the poem
to end all wars,
the one that proves
bullets a likely
cause of death
and death a cause
of sorrow.
The one that points out
connections between
anger and bent fingers,
bent fingers and triggers,
triggers and sorrow,
bent fingers and tears,
anger and sorrow.
The one that says;
to avoid tears
do not bend fingers
but raise hands in air,
wave, clap, embrace,
shake hands, smile, clap,
wave, raise hands in air.
The one that makes it easy.
The one that forgets fingers
obey the shape of the heart.
The one we have all written
at some time or other.

In The Interests Of National Security

It is wrong
to be wrong
unless
you are wrong
while protecting
the right people
from wrong.
Then it is
alright to be wrong
because rulers
have the rights
on what is right
and there's no-one
big enough
to tell a ruler
what is wrong.
Right?

(Wrong)

Los Angeles

If Jesus Was Born Today

If Jesus was born today
it would be in a downtown motel
marked by a helicopter's flashing bulb.
A traffic warden, working late,
would be the first upon the scene.
Later, at the expense of a TV network,
an eminent sociologist,
the host of a chat show
and a controversial author
would arrive with their good wishes
—the whole occasion to be filmed as part of the
'Is This The Son Of God?' one hour special.
Childhood would be a blur of photographs
and speculation
dwindling by His late teens into
'Where Is He Now?' features in Sunday magazines.

If Jesus was thirty today
they wouldn't really care about the public ministry,
they'd be too busy investigating His finances
and trying to prove He had Church or Mafia
connections.
The miracles would be explained by
an eminent and controversial magician,
His claims to be God's Son recognised as
excellent examples of Spoken English
and immediately incorporated into
the O-Level syllabus,
His sinless perfection considered by moral philosophers
as, OK, but a bit repressive.

If Jesus was thirty-one today
He'd be the fly in everyone's ointment—
the sort of controversial person who
stands no chance of eminence.
Communists would expel Him, capitalists
would exploit Him or have Him
smeared by people who know a thing or two about God.
Doctors would accuse Him of quackery,
soldiers would accuse Him of cowardice,
theologians would take Him aside and try
to persuade Him of His non-existence.

If Jesus was thirty-two today we'd have to
end it all. Heretic, fundamentalist, literalist,
puritan, pacifist, non-comformist, we'd take Him
away and quietly end the argument.
But the argument would rumble in the ground
at the end of three days and would break out
and walk around as though death was some bug,
saying 'I am the resurrection and the life . . .
No man cometh to the Father but by me'.
While the magicians researched new explanations
and the semanticists wondered exactly what
He meant by 'I' and 'No man' there would be those
who stand around amused, asking for something
called proof.

Exclusive Pictures

Give us good pictures
of the human torch
which show the skin
burnt like chicken,
bursting like grapes.

It will teach us
to avoid flames.

Give us good film
of the lady on the ledge
as she leaps open mouthed
and hits the streets
like a suicide.

It will teach us
to use stairways.

Give us sharp colour
coverage of the African
troubles. Show us
interesting wounds,
craters in fat and flesh.

It will teach us
not to point guns.

Give us five page spreads
of the airliner that fell
like a pigeon to the ground.
And make sure you get there
before the victims are pulled out.

It will teach
engines to function.

Don't give us
any of that shaky
hand-held stuff
where the trapped children
are smoke-like shapes
and their screams barely audible
beneath the wailing sirens.
Get in there with your lenses
and your appetite for danger
and your hard news head
and give us what we're after.
Make us informed.
Make us feel we're really there.
Provide us with education.
Broaden our backgrounds.
We live in a democracy
and we need to know.

Left Right

Left right Left right
Left right Left right

I was getting worried
Couldn't sleep at night
'Cos I didn't quite know
If I was left or right
So feel my leanings
Test my views
Check my reactions
to the Ten o'Clock News

Should I buy the *Mirror*
Or should I buy the *Sun*
The *Times Literary*
Or the *Guardian*?
Will I be a fascist
If I use the police
Or will I be a commie
If I march for peace?
Who is it I follow
If I'm down on porn
Begin a Foetus Lib
For the not yet born?

Feel my leanings
Test my views
Check my reactions
to the Ten o'Clock News

Am I middle class
Or am I alright
Get me tested
Am I left or right?
Get me tested
Am I left or right?

Send me all the questions
Mail me all the forms
Fix me up a blood test
Tell me all the rules
I've got to know now
Put my mind at rest
Am I of the right
Or am I communist?
Please make me something
I've been nothing too long
I need to find out
If I'm left or wrong.

Watch my language
Hear my views
Check my reactions
To the Six o'Clock News
Am I working class
And am I alright
Get me tested
Am I left or right?
Get me tested
Am I left or right?

They Had It Coming

The South East Asians,
they were made to cry,
Look at their eyes all
narrowed up and ready to bawl.
Black Africans:
Obesity wouldn't suit them.
There's a grace about their
slenderness.
Their children would be naked
without a covering of flies.
Indians are perfect for begging
in ragged clothes
and falling dead on the streets
without too much sensation.
There are so many of them
that death is no longer a problem.
Middle Easterners, South Americans,
they were made to look anguished,
the mother crying to God,
the children just crying.
Earthquakes provide opportunity
for this.
White Westerners were made to laugh
in fast cars with beautiful friends.
They were made to drink and spend money.
Do not disturb the balance of nature.

Wait

These are
the good
old days.

Just wait
and see.

Short Poem

Short poems
are fun.
You can see
at a glance
whether you
like them
or not.

For Georgi Vins, The Day After His Release

Already I'm beginning to wonder
when freedom will lose its bright glow for you.
Today you must be delirious with smiling faces,
open Bible, open street, open door, open gospel,
open church.
But already I'm beginning to wonder
when you'll notice that the palms are thinning out
on the dusty road from Siberia.
I'm beginning to wonder
when you'll see that there are never any fingerprints
in the hotel Gideon.
I'm beginning to wonder
when you'll walk the streets of New York
and whether you'll go out alone.
I'm beginning to wonder
whether you'll hear secret police
whistling tunes in elevators and supermarkets
in a carefully conceived plan
to stop the private ownership of thoughts.
I'm beginning to wonder
when you'll see your first millionaire evangelist
asking for more money to stay on TV
so that he can ask for more money to stay on TV.

I'm beginning to wonder
when you'll pass your first State church
closed by the people.
I'm beginning to wonder
when they'll let you meet the victims of freedom,
persecuted by apathy, exiled within themselves.

Los Angeles

Stuck At Seventeen (Rock 'n' Roll Poem)

Hey mum I'm all grown up
Yet I feel like a kid
Must be something I ate
Or something that you did
I'm going on thirty
And I'm stuck at seventeen
Should be into grey suits
And I'm still wearing jeans

You said that rock 'n' roll
Was an adolescent phase
That sprung up like a spot
And disappeared in days
You said I'd see sense
Then turn into a man
Try Tchaikovsky
Throw my records in the can

But I'm all grown up and I'm stuck at seventeen
You'll never make me different from the way I've
always been
I'm all grown up and I'm stuck at seventeen
I'm an innocent delinquent and rock 'n' rolling being

You showed me winklepickers
and the cramping of the toes
Losses of employment
Through the colour of me clothes

Possible delinquency
By wearing tapered jeans
Effects of rock 'n' roll
Upon impressionable teens

You really did your best
To try and make me get well
With those sensible shoes
And the tubes of Trugel
With the nice sons of friends
and some hymns with a beat
And modern brown sandals
To give me healthy feet.

But I'm all grown up and I'm stuck at seventeen
You'll never make me different from the way I've
always been
I'm all grown up and I'm stuck at seventeen
I'm an innocent delinquent and a rock 'n' rolling being

But nothin' really worked
I'm in a leather jacket
I tried wearin' ties but
my neck couldn't hack it
Don't wait for Steve mother
He's never gonna grow
He's gonna be like Johnny
And just Go, Go, Go.

Not

Thick around
the middle,
not fat.
Receding,
not going bald.
Tired eyes,
not failing sight.
Maturing features,
not wrinkled skin.
Growing older,
not dying.

Waterlow, Massachusetts.

The Appeal

Don't give them your money.
They don't really need it.
It'll only create problems.
We need helpless people
and money wipes them out.
Too much food
and they'll have to
bring in the slimming pills.
Too much success
and they'll have to
fly in psychiatrists.
These folk have found the simple life,
the open-air life, the life
unencumbered by possessions,
by status.
Don't export the
curse of affluence
to the Third World.
They'll only become like us
or, if we give too freely,
we'll become like them.

Christmas Is Really For The Children

Christmas is really
for the children.
Especially for children
who like animals, stables,
stars and babies wrapped
in swaddling clothes.
Then there are wise men,
kings in fine robes,
humble shepherds and a
hint of rich perfume.

Easter is not really
for the children
unless accompanied by
a cream filled egg.
It has whips, blood, nails,
a spear and allegations
of body snatching.
It involves politics, God
and the sins of the world.
It is not good for people
of a nervous disposition.
They would do better to
think on rabbits, chickens
and the first snowdrop
of spring.

Or they'd do better to
wait for a re-run of
Christmas without asking
too many questions about
what Jesus did when he grew up
or whether there's any connection.

Birth

I didn't ask
to be born.
I wasn't even
there to ask.
When you are born
you can ask for
anything.
Almost anything.
You cannot ask
to be unborn.
If you do
there is very little
that can be done.
I didn't ask
to be born.
I was under age
at the time.
My parents had
to decide
on my behalf.
I'm glad that
I was born.
You have to be born
to be glad.

History Lesson

History repeats itself.
Has to.
No-one listens.

Letter Bomb

Take care.
It is not
always possible
to detect them
at first glance.
They weigh as much
as circulars
or income tax demands.
Take care.
Normally they start
with a Dear where
a Dearest used to be.
They go on to say
something about not
knowing how to put it.
They put it.
They hope you're not hurt.
You are.
Take care.
Do not plunge the package
into a brine-soaked
handkerchief.
Withdraw.
Call for assistance.

'It's all for the best.'
'Time is a great healer.'

After You'd Gone

No-one
like you.
That then
the pleasure.
That now
the pain.

Washington D.C.

Truth

There's no
such thing
as truth.

No.
Not even
    this.

People Who Die

People who die in disasters,
like people who get themselves murdered,
are not really people.
Their photographs prove it;
always slightly out of focus
taken in gardens we do not know,
resorts we would not visit.
They come from towns
we have never been to.
They leave relations
with funny names.
They led 'quiet lives'
and had 'few close friends'.
People who are reported missing
like people who fall dead in the street
are not really people.
Like extra-terrestrial life
they never come from your street.
Like extra-terrestrial life
they are news, but only for a day.

Jingles

(*i*)
Absence makes the
heart grow fonder.

Get ABSENCE.

(*ii*)
Out of sight is
out of mind.
Girl, you are
outtasight.

Five Hundred Million Pounds

The Earl of Grosvenor
has five hundred million pounds.
He is honeymooning in Hawaii.
He has five hundred million pounds
and he still has to honeymoon
in the world.
He has married Natalia.
She is not my sort of girl.
Five hundred million pounds
and he marries someone
who is not my sort of girl.
The Earl of Grosvenor
carries a black case
in his right hand.
Five hundred million pounds
and he still has to carry
a black case in his right hand.
It is probably heavy.
He will probably sweat.
Damp patches will form
beneath his arms
as if he were a construction worker
or an unemployed gentleman
carrying a black case.
I expect his shoes hurt sometimes.
I expect he forgets his handkerchief.
I expect he wonders whether Natalia
really loves him.

I expect he wonders what it would be like
to have only four hundred and fifty
million pounds.
The Earl of Grosvenor takes off.
He wonders whether the engines will catch fire.
He knows you can't pay engines off.
He knows that the ocean is indifferent to millionaires.
Five hours in the air and he is restless.
Five hundred million pounds and he is restless.

The Photographs

They take them away.
That's what's so frightening.
One moment they're happy,
as the photographs show,
and then they are taken
behind the tall walls,
along cold passageways,
to the places we do not go.
What happens next is
a medical secret
but has to do with ageing
in a very short time.
What happens next is
the mortician's secret.
One moment they're happy,
as the photographs show,
and then they are
words carved in stone
on freshly broken ground.
Look at the photographs.
Look at their eyes.
Look at their smiles.
IT'S BEHIND YOU! we shout,
it's behind you.

Everything

Looks aren't everything.
Luxury's not everything.
Money's not everything.
Health is not everything.
Success is not everything.
Happiness is not everything.
Even everything is not everything.
There's more to life than everything.

Creed

We believe in Marxfreudanddarwin.
We believe everything is OK
as long as you don't hurt anyone,
to the best of your definition of hurt,
and to the best of your knowledge.

We believe in sex before during
and after marriage.
We believe in the therapy of sin.
We believe that adultery is fun.
We believe that sodomy's OK
We believe that taboos are taboo.

We believe that everything's getter better
despite evidence to the contrary.
The evidence must be investigated.
You can prove anything with evidence.

We believe there's something in horoscopes,
UFO's and bent spoons;
Jesus was a good man just like Buddha
Mohammed and ourselves.
He was a good moral teacher although we think
his good morals were bad.

We believe that all religions are basically the same,
at least the one that we read was.
They all believe in love and goodness.
They only differ on matters of
creation sin heaven hell God and salvation.

We believe that after death comes The Nothing
because when you ask the dead what happens
they say Nothing.
If death is not the end, if the dead have lied,
then it's compulsory heaven for all
excepting perhaps Hitler, Stalin and Genghis Khan.

We believe in Masters and Johnson.
What's selected is average.
What's average is normal.
What's normal is good.

We believe in total disarmament.
We believe there are direct links between
warfare and bloodshed.
Americans should beat their guns into tractors
and the Russians would be sure to follow.

We believe that man is essentially good.
It's only his behaviour that lets him down.
This is the fault of society.
Society is the fault of conditions.
Conditions are the fault of society.

We believe that each man must find the truth
that is right for him.
Reality will adapt accordingly.
The universe will readjust. History will alter.
We believe that there is no absolute truth
excepting the truth that there is no absolute truth.

We believe in the rejection of creeds.

UP TO DATE

The Portrait Of The Artist

I was deprived.
I never had the unhappy childhood
necessary for greatness.
The worst things that happened
were shopping with mother,
unfinished homework
and the ghost beneath the bed.
My one regret in life
that I was not born
on the bad side of town.
At fourteen I wanted to be
Heavyweight Champion Of The World
but failed to make the scales
and had no previous criminal record.
I could've been the next John Lennon
but my parents couldn't misunderstand me.
My first novel dried up
through lack of trauma,
my cupboards had no skeletons,
there were no ghosts to exorcise.
Now I'm going for the Poet.
I'm looking for the mess
that could be the key,
the chip that could be the spur.
If only things had been different.
If only I could have been like the rest.
All I asked of life was
some poverty to flee from
and a pit to climb out of.

Dial-A-Poem Is Temporarily Out Of Order

All poems have been cancelled today
because of the national poetry strike.
Poets are demanding equal rights
with rock stars and saints.
They want
to be
paid by the
column inch
rather than
the
word.
They want overtime rates for
nocturnal inspiration,
danger money for love affairs that end.
Poets are demanding a closed shop.
Rhymsters and graffiti artists
will not be admitted,
nor any employee of Hallmark Cards.
Poets want pens that don't run in your pocket.
Poets want bigger cigarette packets for epic verse.
Poets want repeat fees for every line memorised.
Poets want better thinking conditions.
All poems have been cancelled today.
Pens and typewriters lie idle.
The general public are advised
to stock up with alternative forms of literature.
All poems have been cancelled.

No-one notices the sun rise,
no-one hears the wind.
Somewhere a poet falls in love
but he can't put it into words.

It's Great To Be Back

It's great to be back
in your cute little country
where the assassins roam
and the murderers play.
You're all so American,
it's just like TV.
I love your accent.
Say something for me.
Say something else.
Everyone is friendly
in your wonderful country.
Everyone helps me
pull out my money.
Everyone wants me
to have a nice day.
Everyone wants me
to come back real soon.

It's great to be back
amongst your skyscrapers.
The sky needs scraping.
And I just love
your wandering freeways
and your ancient cities
dating back to before the television,
before the wireless.
I want to see history.
I want to see where Marilyn slept
and where Disney dreamt.

I want to see where Errol swung
and Dia Maggio scored.
I want to see the castles
of Anaheim
and the oldest restaurant
in Hollywood.
I want to see the tomb
of the great king Elvis.

It's great to be back
in your cute big country
where the hugh hefners roam
and the centrefolds play.
I just adore your policemen
with their pink smiling faces
and their snub nosed guns.
They are helpful with directions.
They tell people where to go.

Moscow Winter

All our still lives
the ice has whipped our skin
and left us frozen.
Heads bowed and shoulders curled
we forced our silhouettes
across the landscape.
We must walk along
the well trodden paths
for fear of slipping,
for fear of disappearing.
All around us the snow
lies watching,
a history of small blows,
hardening into a rock
that becomes our habitation.

Mikhail Suslov Formerly The Second Most Powerful Member Of The Soviet Politburo
Lies In State In Moscow

With eyes shut
to ideology,
hands too stiff
to launch the
first strike,
he lies in satin
and flowers.
All redness
has gone.
His skin has
become neutral.
At last
he is one with
Stalin's millions,
at last he has
climbed down into
the people.
His greatness has
been mislaid
through some
mechanical fault.
He can command
only stares.
He is meek.
He will inherit earth.

Assassin

The assassin was
a most ordinary man.
Ask his teacher.
Ask his mother.
Ask his girlfriend.
Ask the doorman.
And it was on
a most ordinary day
that he slid the bolt
that slid the metal
through the cloth
and through the skin.
It felt most ordinary.
Almost no effort.
As easy as blinking.
And when they led him
to the cellroom
he felt ordinary.
He felt hungry.
This did not feel like history.
This did not feel like news.
This did not feel like
the end of an era.

The Serpent

The serpent is more subtle.
He is more subtle
than a rhinoceros
who cannot slither up unsuspectingly.
He is more subtle
than a lion
who cannot swing from branches.
He is more subtle
than a terrapin,

      a goat,
more subtle than truth.
You think he is a stick
until you collect him
for firewood.
You think he is a leaf
until he bends down
to kiss.
You think he is a stone,
           a tree,
           a good idea,
           your true self.
The serpent has more beauty.
He amazes you with his colour
which speaks with the sun.
He amazes you with his grace.
If you have not been told
you will want to take him in your hand,
you will want to take him home.

Beat Poem

I never met Kerouac.
He was off the road
before I got on.
I met Ginsberg
and he told me
'don't cling to ideas'.
He took a handkerchief
and dabbed snot
from my nose.
I said 'sorry'.
Ginsberg said;
'don't cling to ideas'.
I met the crazy Corso.
The first thing
he asked me was
'have you written
home to your mother?'
I spent an afternoon
getting him to
the evening on time.
He told me not to
worry about the bomb.
He said the extinction
of mankind could be
the next big step
in evolution.
I never met Ferlinghetti.
The City Light was always out
when I was on the North Beach.

I did meet Dylan though.
He was small
and had a wet handshake
and dark teeth.

When Your Revolution Is Over

When your revolution is over
When your revolution is over
Will you rebuild the city?
Will you rebuild the city?

Will you drain away the tears?
Will you retouch every scar?
Will you mend the broken hearts?
Will you find the stolen years?
Will you light up the blind eye?
Will you raise up the dead?

Ah.

Then I do not want
I do not want
Your revolution.

Never Talk About Him
(A. S. Turner, Killed in Action 1918)

never talk about him
never say his name
germans gone and done it
put metal in his head
gone and stole his blood
gone and stole his breath
put him in the mud house
put him in the ground
never talk about him
never say his name
never play at soldiers
leave him where he lives
leave him in my mind
germans gone and done it
put metal in his head
gone and stole his blood
gone and stole his breath

Unknown Soldier

Was he old?
No, not old.
Twenty or so,
no more.
An officer?
A private,
no stripes,
front line.
Decorations?
Stone over
his body,
medal for
his mother.
Was he famous?
No,
but he went at
the bidding
of the famous.
What say
the records?
Only
that his records
were lost
in the world's next war.

Whose Grave Is The Ocean

Whose grave is the ocean
whose roof gulls skim,
and wind thresh.
Whose words were soaked
and whose eyes
were dulled by salt.
Guided by stars
with hearts fixed on home,
whose inheritance was none.
Down beneath froth
with the tangled rust of glory;
beyond all horizons,
amongst the kingdom not their own.
The ocean shifts its weight
as if pushed by a prayer
and the sunken socket
eyes the surface broken light.

Whose grave is the ocean
whose resurrection sprays.
Whose trumpet cracks the water
with a gilded flash of joy.

The News And Weather

A man shot a man who shot a man who shot a man
Said it wasn't murder it just went off in his hand
We got a bigger bomb than the one we had before
On the Middle East border there wasn't any score
Some people starved to death in a city far away
A man in a suit will read the weather for today
A man in a suit will read the weather for today

A spokesman said he could not comment at the time
A friend of a friend said the rumour was a lie
The next door neighbour always thought that he was
                                                    funny
The man who guessed the draw was given lots of
                                                    money
The corrupt M.P. said he'd nothing more to say
A man in a suit will read the weather for today
A man in a suit will read the weather for today

The star of thirty films has just cast his fifth wife
The man who killed children must stay indoors for life
The financial index is falling down again
Pence to the dollar to the mark to the yen
Tobacco and petrol and the price you'll have to pay
A man in a suit will read the weather for today
A man in a suit will read the weather for today

At the football match it was the crowd who went and
                                                    lost

The team managers are trying to estimate the cost
The little girl went missing only three days ago
Don't travel by train because they're on a go-slow
A leading tennis player has admitted that he's gay
A man in a suit will read the weather for today
A man in a suit will read the weather for today

Policemen say watch out for strangers at your door
Ring this number if you've seen this man before
Another soldier died but he didn't have a girl
There's been a great disaster the biggest in the world
Yet down at the zoo the woolly bears come out to play
A man in a suit will read the weather for today
A man in a suit will read the weather for today

A two minute warning will follow this newscast
You'll hear a high pitched noise, then you'll hear a blast
The windows will go missing, you'll be blinded by a
                                                    light
But if you remain calm everything will be alright
Some of you may notice that your skin will peel away
A man in a suit will read the weather for today
A man in a suit will read the weather for today.

The Prophet

You didn't stone the prophet.
The odd joke or two maybe.
Impersonations, a cartoon.
A hint of 'trouble in the brain'.
But you didn't stone him,
there are no bruises, no breaks.
You didn't stone the prophet.
He's alive and walking.
Not on TV much, not on radio,
but in the countryside, somewhere.
(I saw a photograph).
You didn't stone the prophet.
But then look at the trouble
you've had with martyrs.
Everyone wants to hear them.
The dead are so hard to shut up.
You didn't stone the prophet.
You just told us that he had problems.
Nothing that a prostitute
or a psychiatrist couldn't cure.
He's too young and old.
Too fascist socialist.
No, you didn't stone the prophet.
You gave him the microphone
every now and then
and supplied us with experts
to add some perspective.
The offical view is
                    Don't Panic.

No, you didn't stone the prophet.
You said there were crazies like him
around in ancient Rome
but Italy survives.
The official view was
                    Don't Panic.
You didn't stone the prophet.
You didn't even censor him.
You didn't put him in prison.
You just put him in perspective.

I Looked Down

I looked down and I saw you were not looking
I looked down and I saw you were not looking
You were building a tower that stretched to the moon
You were building a statue inscribed with your name
You were making up lies and calling them truths
You were losing the blood of your brothers and sisters
You were burying the poor for having no money
You were flattering the rich for loving themselves
You were killing the black for not being whiter
You were killing your wife for not being a lover
And I'm turning my face
    I'm turning my face
    I'm turning my face
    from you

I looked down and I saw you were not looking
I looked down and I saw you were not looking
You invented someone and you gave him my name
You invented another and you called him the same
You heard what I said but you tried not to listen
You said you were special no need for attention
You said you were okay but you just wanted time
You said in the future you might give me a call
You bowed at the altar of your five sacred senses
You worshipped the power of a skull full of brain
And I'm turning my face
    I'm turning my face
    I'm turning my face
    from you

I looked down and I saw you were not looking
I looked down and I saw you were not looking
You were digging the ground to find where you came
                                                from
You were looking in tubes to see how it happened
You were watching in zoos to learn good and evil
You were having a vote for the new golden rule
You were laying foundations for the new earthly
                                            kingdom
You were judging the bad with the wrath of your trigger
You were laughing at wise men and crowning the fools
You were selling a love that was no love at all
And I'm turning my face
    I'm turning my face
    I'm turning my face
    from you

I looked down and I saw you were not looking
I looked down and I saw you were not looking
You were paying the camera to rape your young
                                        daughters
You were having affairs with adult publications
You were paying accountants to steal from the peasants
You were using your tongue with the force of a bullet
You were painting your lies in the colour of paper
You were learning a language that would hide all your
                                                    sins
You were making yourself of the world's leading
                                            religion
You were meeting the devil to get an opinion
And I'm turning my face
    I'm turning my face
    I'm turning my face
    from you

163

The City Without Love

In the city without love
buildings turn their backs on you,
the night air hangs around
like an enemy in waiting.
You hope you will not fall sick
in the city without love
because the mortician
is nearer than the surgeon
and the citizens are lazy.
You are from the bad side of the family,
your words come out as nonsense,
your questions are annoying,
in the city without love.
In the city without love
you are walking on the wrong street
at the wrong time of night.
This is where the rough boys live,
this is the haunted room,
this is where the strangers stare,
this is the city without love.

Here Am I

This is my flesh.
I give it to you.
These are my thoughts,
and this is my work.
Here are my faults.
Here is the fear
I discuss with myself.
Here are my good jokes,
here are my bad ones.
The flesh is falling apart,
it will have to do.
The thoughts are uncontrollable
some of them hate each other.

Here is my sweat,
and my decay,
the face only mirrors see.
This is my love
and my lack of love.
Here is my laughter.
Here are the years.
Here am I.

Spiritus

I used to think of you
as a symphony
neatly structured,
full of no surprises.
Now I see you as
a saxophone solo
blowing wildly
into the night,
a tongue of fire,
flicking in unrepeated
                patterns.

Not Yet

The angels are impatient.
They pace the corridors of heaven
wondering if it is to be today
or today
or today.
Doctors' reports have been studied.
It could be now. There's every chance.
Pulse rate. Blood test. The inevitability.
Someone says you're long overdue.
Suggests help. The angels frown.
They hear you kicking.
They sense your longing.
They know this is normal.
At night you hear their feet
somewhere beyond the screen.
You try reaching out
but it is not yet.
You are not yet.
Not yet for you.

I Am

I'm a hastily written ending
I'm a punchline in bad taste
I'm an argument in reserve
I'm the fact that theories hate

I'm the only thing not mentioned
I'm the catch that there must be
I'm a robbery with violence
I'm the one you would not see

I'm the bad dream that has to come true
I'm obsolescence built in
I'm the door you cannot look behind
I'm as original as sin

I'm the problem that changes the plan
I'm the unexpected guest
I'm the confusion of philosophers
I'm the well known factor X.

All You Need Is Hate

Alan hated soldiers and teachers
and politicians, policemen and bankers.
Alan was full of hate for such people.
Poured his hate into poems.
Threw the poems at audiences
who sat bleeding in their seats,
words hanging from holes in their skin.
Hate them, he shouted, boot stomping
the boards.
Hate them. Hate them.
Alan, I said. Alan.
Hate hate, Alan, I said. Hate
                              hate.
It's the only hate worth having Alan
and it comes by another name.

Once More With Feeling

Sandy, when you were girlish
You called love from your heart
It came in all innocence
To ask when it could start

It began around your lips
It worked from heart to head
It brought you to ecstasy
At least that's what you said

But then you found the motions
Which love had brought you free
Were sold out on the market
You could fake it for a fee

So you put your love on call
It responded to your shout
It thought of mystic union
You thought of in and out

Chorus
So it's
Once more with feeling
Once more like it was
Once more for the money
Once more for the boss
Once more for the customer
And once more for the rent
Once more for the madam
Once more as though it's meant.

You became good at loving
Or something by its name
You went about your business
You stepped out on the game

And now it's just an action
That helps the coin to drop
Some simulated feelings
Once more from the top

The love left you long ago
Called out once too often
Your body was a liar
No tenderness could soften

Ecstasy that went as well
It walked away abused
Your nerves had lost their endings
Through being over used

Chorus
So it's
Once more with feeling etc.

You think of love sometimes
Though you've forgotten how
You call it when you're lonely
It does not hear you now

It looks so much like business
You can't tell them apart
Though one comes from the pelvis
And one comes from the heart

Chorus
So it's
Once more with feeling etc.

Voices

I love you.
Do you?
I love you.
I'm glad.
I love you.
I know you do.
I love you.
Thank you.
Do you love me?
Who couldn't?
Do you love me?
Doesn't it show?
Do you love me?
I admire you.
Do you love me?
There's no-one else.
I love you.
I remember.

Decision Making

The old age pensioner is
like the unborn child.
He is wrinkled and curved
and thrashes in his elastic cage.
He moves in his sea of darkness
and looks beautiful to the camera.
The old age pensioner does not understand
the modern world and needs help
with decision making.
Like an unborn child his spending power is small,
his voice is mute.
Like an unborn child
the old age pensioner does not win elections
or foreign contracts,
or athletic events.
He is not a member of any recognised union.
He has to be helped with his decision making.
He has to be advised that it is not wise
to be unwanted, helpless.
The unwanted are a pang,
they are a blush.
It is painful to be unwanted.
Better the short pain, he has to be advised,
than the lingering ache.
The old age pensioner is like the unborn child.
He has to be helped with decision making.

British Rail Regrets

British Rail regrets
having to regret.
British Rail regrets
it cannot spell.
British Rail regrets
the chalk ran out.
British Rail regrets
that due to a staff shortage
there will be no-one
to offer regrets.
British Rail regrets,
but will not be sending
flowers or tributes.
British Rail regrets
the early arrival
of your train.
This was due to industrious action.
British Rail regrets
that because of a work-to-rule
by our tape machine
this is a real person.
British Rail regrets
the cheese shortage
in your sandwich.
This is due to
a points failure.
The steward got
three out of ten.

British Rail regrets.
Tears flow from beneath
the locked doors of staff rooms.
Red-eyed ticket collectors
offer comfort
to stranded passengers.
Angry drivers threaten
to come out in sympathy
with the public.
British Rail regrets.
That's why its members
are permanently dressed in black.
That's why porters stand around
as if in a state of shock.
That's why Passenger Information
is off the hook.

British Rail regrets
that due to the shortage of regrets
there will be a train.